LEADING A TRANSFORMING COMMUNITY

STUDY GUIDE

Six Sessions for Personal Reflection, Group Conversation, and Next Steps

RUTH HALEY BARTON

ivp

An imprint of InterVarsity Press
Downers Grove, Illinois

InterVarsity Press
P.O. Box 1400 | Downers Grove, IL 60515-1426
ivpress.com | email@ivpress.com

InterVarsity Press® is the publishing division of InterVarsity Christian Fellowship/USA®. For more information, visit intervarsity.org.

Cover design: Amy Cerra
Interior design: Jeanna Wiggins

ISBN 978-1-5140-0150-9 (print) | ISBN 978-1-5140-0151-6 (digital)

Printed in the United States of America ♾

Library of Congress Cataloging-in-Publication Data
Names: Barton, R. Ruth, 1960- author | Barton, R. Ruth, 1960-. Leading a transforming community
Title: Leading a transforming community study guide : six sessions for personal reflection, group conversation, and next steps / Ruth Haley Barton.
Description: Downers Grove, IL : IVP, [2026] | Includes bibliographical references.
Identifiers: LCCN 2026017431 (print) | LCCN 2026017432 (ebook) | ISBN 9781514001509 paperback | ISBN 9781514001516 ebook
Subjects: LCSH: Christian leadership–Study and teaching | Communities–Religious aspects–Christianity–Study and teaching | Spiritual life–Christianity–Study and teaching | Church group work–Study and teaching
Classification: LCC BV652.1 .B372 2026 (print) | LCC BV652.1 (ebook)
LC record available at https://lccn.loc.gov/2026017431
LC ebook record available at https://lccn.loc.gov/2026017432

A catalog record for this book is available from the Library of Congress.

32 31 30 29 28 27 26 | 8 7 6 5 4 3 2 1

Christianity needs to clarify and exemplify
realistic methods for human transformation.
It must show how ordinary individuals who make up
the human race today can become, through the
grace of Christ, a love-filled, effective,
and powerful community.

Dallas Willard

CONTENTS

INTRODUCTION

Spiritual formation is about shaping the inner person in such a way that the words and deeds of Christ naturally flow from us. It is the inward transformation of the self that makes it easy and natural to do the things Jesus said.

Dallas Willard

One of the great mysteries of my life growing up as a pastor's kid was the fact that many adults in the churches I attended—some of whom had been attending for many years—were just not changing. I couldn't help but notice that many of them remained selfish, stuck in their ways, and spiritually lifeless. I wondered, *How can someone go to church year after year, read the Bible, listen to sermons, participate in small groups—and yet change very little?*

And then as the years went by, I sometimes wondered the same thing about myself!

THE PROMISE OF SPIRITUAL TRANSFORMATION

I wonder what your experiences in Christian communities have been. Did you find them transforming or deforming or a little bit of both? No matter what our experience has been up to this point, the promise that we—sin-scarred human beings that we are—can become like Christ is one of the great promises of the good news Jesus brought and the very gospel we preach. How can your community become a community that not only champions but *embodies* the truth that spiritual transformation is central to the message of the gospel and therefore central to the mission of the church? This study guide is designed to help you find out! It will facilitate deeper sharing among those seeking to lead out together from authentic desire, vision, and calling, *and* it is designed to help you identify clear next steps you can take in your setting in response to what you have read. Each session in this guide corresponds to different assigned parts of the book and includes four elements—the first that takes place on your own and three distinct movements that take place when your group gets together.

1. ***Personal reflection (before you meet with the group).*** Take time to read and reflect personally on the themes found in the assigned portion of *Leading a Transforming Community* using the guidance given. This is an important step for everyone who wants to lead with authenticity from his or her soul, and it is important that groups of leaders seeking to cultivate transforming communities are *connected* and *listening to one another spiritually* as a significant part of their preparation for guiding others. The goal for these personal reflections is that each person would come to the group conversations prepared to engage with heart, soul, mind, and strength, rather than just speaking "off the cuff" or engaging primarily in an academic fashion.
2. ***Sharing and listening.*** Start your conversations with a bit of silence, a prayer, a lectio divina reading, or simply checking in with each other using a question like, "Where have you experienced consolation and desolation this week?" "Where did you experience God with you today?" or "Where are you coming from/what are you needing to set aside in order to be fully present in this conversation?" Then, take time for each person to share their personal reflections in response to what they have read; this will prepare each person to engage thoughtfully in prayerful discussion about "what these things might mean" for you and your community. It is impossible to overstate how important starting with personal sharing is to the process of discerning what God is doing in and among you regarding

the possibility of becoming a transforming community. This may take anywhere from fifteen to thirty minutes, depending on the size of the group and the fullness of the sharing, and it should not become a discussion. Clarifying questions and supportive words or gestures are welcome, but in this section, just let people's sharing stand as valuable and important to the group's process.

3. ***Prayerful discussion.*** Thank everyone for what they have shared before moving on to the discussion questions provided for that session. While the first part of the conversation is characterized by sharing and listening without much dialogue, this part of the session welcomes dialogue back and forth—even vigorous dialogue!
4. ***Identify next steps*** in becoming a transforming community. The goal here is that as you conclude the session and before you depart from one another, your group would identify one to three *concrete next steps* you can all agree on and record them. (More than three will probably not be realistic.) Also, identify who will be responsible for leading out on whatever steps you have identified, who needs to be consulted, who needs to be kept informed, and how you will report back to the group on progress and/or challenges. You may even want to identify an optimal time frame for accomplishing each step.

I have also included encouragement to take time to pray for your community at the end of each session, leaving it open for you to do this in different ways each time, if you would like to get creative. You may want to jot down prayer requests that you can return to as you pray for your community throughout the week.

Sometimes a session will bring to the surface more than can be handled fully in the allotted time frame. Do not panic if this happens and try to avoid being too rigid about how quickly you move through this process. Be alert to a spirit of urgency and pushing just to get through the session; instead, be sensitive to the Spirit and to each other about what is really needed. *Always leave the option open to take more time with a particular session if the group needs it.* Knowing this is a possibility will help everyone stay more relaxed in the process. You could even plan from the very beginning to have two meetings per session—the first meeting could be to share personal reflections and engage the questions for conversation and then the second session could be to brainstorm and decide on next steps. This option might be especially helpful if you are adding this process to regularly scheduled meetings that include other agenda items.

ON THE JOURNEY TOGETHER

Keep in mind that the journey of spiritual transformation, if fully embraced, will take us to the deepest places in our personal lives and in our shared humanity. We don't bring up knotty issues to be controversial but, rather, to be open about what contributes to transformation and deformation in community. We will not always agree on everything, but the willingness to have rigorous discussions that result in mutual influence are part and parcel of the transformational journey. Many of us in the Transforming Center would look back and say that these mutually influencing conversations and the ability to "stay with it" are what has changed us in the deepest ways.

When you come across a theological point that makes you want to rise up in protest or engage in theological debate, consider that this might be a place where God is knocking on some closed door of your heart, a place where you may have locked God (and other people) out and locked yourself in. I invite you *not* to give in to reactionary responses, argumentation, or even the urge to "defend the faith." God is perfectly capable of doing that. Instead, breathe, calm yourself, and try to keep your heart open. Choose to be curious. You don't have to agree with everything you've read; all you need to do in such moments is try and open the door a crack to wonder why it matters to the transformational journey. See if the place where you find yourself resisting is something you feel God nudging you to reflect on more deeply.

Transforming communities do not happen by accident—they must be *led* by pastors, priests, and spiritual leaders of intentional communities who are convinced this is what they are being called to cultivate, who are intentional and wise about navigating whatever changes are needed, and who are grounded in strong love, vibrant vision, and courageous conviction. There is so much in our world these days that works against the patient, plodding, mysterious process of spiritual transformation that becoming a community that supports and catalyzes it will be a major sea change for many. But as the apostle Paul writes, ". . . that we may present everyone mature [transformed] in Christ. For this I toil and strive with all the energy that he powerfully inspires within me" (Colossians 1:28-29).

I wish I could be with you as you embark on the journey of becoming a transforming community. I wish I could reflect alongside you, hear your questions, share in your excitement as you identify your next steps, and feel the wind of the Spirit blow through the room. But since that is not possible, I offer you this conversation guide, trusting Jesus to join you on your road between the now and the not-yet, revealing his presence, his peace, and his purposes for your community.

Session 1

LONGING FOR MORE IN COMMUNITY

The entire life of a good Christian
is in fact an exercise in holy desire.

SAINT AUGUSTINE

THE JOURNEY TO BECOMING a transforming community is nothing more and nothing less than a journey of desire—so that's where we begin. The whole point of chapters one and two of *Leading a Transforming Community* is to create space for you to tell the truth about church, to put you in touch with your own spiritual desires regarding community, and to give your group permission to have a conversation about desire in the context of your own community's life.

READ AND REFLECT

Prior to your meeting, read and reflect on chapters one and two, paying attention to:

- where you resonate strongly,
- where you feel resistance,
- what seems like a stirring of the Holy Spirit, and
- what questions you find yourself asking and wondering about.

You may want to use different colored highlighters to keep track of these experiences, or make notes in the margins, or keep a notebook or a journal for ease of sharing when your group gets together.

- What is the truth you need to tell about church and community—past and present?

- What kinds of community experiences have been most transforming for you? Which ones have wounded or deformed you? What kind of help and support have you received for processing these experiences, or have you just "moved on" without processing them at all? Speak to God about this as we begin our exploration of transforming community. (Any or all of this can remain between you and God unless you choose to share it, but it is good to be aware that our own and others' past experiences will be present in the room whether they have been shared or not.)

- These days, where do you turn for help and support in seeking deeper levels of change and transformation? What does that look like?

- What desires are you in touch with right now pertaining to your own spiritual life and your journey of transformation? (If you notice that getting in touch with desire is difficult for you, chapter one of *Sacred Rhythms* can provide helpful guidance.)

- How easy or difficult is it for you to trust that there are desires God has placed within your heart (individually and collectively) that God promises to meet (Psalm 37:4)? If you still have doubt or discomfort about the role of desire in the spiritual life, take time to read the biblical stories referred to on pages 10-11, noticing how Jesus interacted with people in these conversations and what the outcome was.

WHEN YOUR GROUP GETS TOGETHER

Sharing and Listening

Share as much or as little as you would like from your personal reflections above. To share at a personal level like this will be foundational for your group's ability to move forward in leading a transforming community, because we cannot lead others into places where we have not been willing to go ourselves. Hold safe space for each person—no judgment, no fixing or problem solving, no commentary. Just gratitude for what each person is choosing to share of themselves. Be sure to create space for each person to share while at the same time assuring people it is always permissible to pass. Depending on how many people are in your group and how deep they go in their sharing, this could take between twenty and thirty minutes—and it should!

Prayerful Discussion (with Dialogue)

1. How easy or difficult, normal or uncomfortable is it for you to talk about desire? How might you create space and opportunity (as Jesus did) for individuals to speak honestly about their spiritual desires?

2. What is one desire you could each name for what you hope for in your community? In your experience, does Christian community make us better or busier? Does it really make a difference when it comes to the transformation of human beings into the image of Christ?

3. How do you respond to the description of the relationship between spiritual formation and mission found in chapter one (pages 12-15)?

   Where have you experienced this false dichotomy to be at work, and how does the approach outlined here both in words (pages 13-14) and in the graphic (page 14) bring the two together? What difference would it make if your community embraced this?

4. How do you understand and experience the relationship between private devotion and life together in community in our spiritual transformation? Is there one that tends to be emphasized more than the other in your tradition?

5. Most Christians would affirm that they desire to discern and do the will of God. In Romans 12:2 Paul identifies a cause-and-effect relationship between our spiritual transformation and our ability to discern and do the will of God. How do you respond to this? Is this a new thought for you?

6. Chapter two opens with a description of stability within community as a practice that is significant to our spiritual transformation. Where have you experienced this? Has stability been part of any tradition you've been a part of?

7. Do you agree or disagree with the statement that stability is "a vow we make to God in the context of the life we have been given because (counterintuitively) to accept one's life as it is, is to begin to find freedom"? What are your thoughts about how stability in community contributes to our transformation?

8. Dr. Elaine Heath distinguishes between tradition (small *t*) and the great Tradition (capital *T*) of following a God who is always making all things new. What is your tradition? How have you experienced following the great Tradition in your own life?

9. What would it look like for your community to follow the God who is always making all things new? Where is God stirring up something new in your community right now?

10. Consider the idea that community is about "coming together in unity" around something everyone agrees is important—in this case our commitment to deeper levels of spiritual transformation in Christ. What would it look like for your community to come together more intentionally around a commitment to spiritual transformation? Be as specific as possible.

NEXT STEPS IN TRANSFORMING COMMUNITY

The second half of chapter two describes one church's journey toward coming together in unity around their commitment to spiritual formation and all that entailed—particularly from its leaders. What would be next steps you could take from this leadership conversation into the rest of the community? It might be something as simple as preaching on the role of desire in the spiritual life and then structuring the kind of conversation you've been able to have among yourselves as leaders in such a way as to engage and include others. Another idea might be to consider entering into a season of listening to yourself and your own deep desires as well as creating opportunities for others in your community to reflect on their longings and desires. Go slowly. Listen deeply. Don't rush to answers. Ask clarifying questions. Seek to be as accurate as possible in understanding and capturing what people say. You may need to simplify your community's schedule or even eliminate some of your normal programming and activities in order to create time and space for a year of listening in which you organize your community's life around personal reflection and communal conversation.

You will also need to consider what your role as leaders is in all of this. What needs to happen *in you* to prepare you to lead others? This might even begin to form one of your early next steps. There is no need to rush things, so resist the urge to be overachievers. Instead, do something before you do everything, and be utterly realistic about what's possible. Although you will each be taking your own notes, I suggest appointing a scribe who will take the "official" notes and capture them in a master list at the back of this guide.

PRAY FOR OUR COMMUNITY

Take time to pray together for your journey toward becoming a transforming community, or name and jot down concerns that you commit to prayer until you meet again.

Session 2

THEOLOGY THAT SHAPES THE SOUL

Be transformed by the renewing of the mind,
so that you may discern what is the will of God.

Romans 12:2

Transforming community begins with desire and continues with clear vision and then teaching that illuminates the path to true change. We need good information because without it grave mistakes can be made, but that is only the beginning. Authentic change and transformation require guidance for engaging in the behaviors, relationships, practices, and experiences that help us internalize truth in ways that change how we respond in the world. One of the reasons some resist embracing spiritual transformation as a priority, rather than seeing it merely as an elective, is that they are not ready for change at this level.

Here is an example of the difference between believing things at a cognitive level and true change. I am a nervous flier and have been for years. When I have a trip coming up that requires air travel, I dread it for days. At takeoff, my palms sweat. During the flight I feel every little bit of turbulence as a shock through my body, and my heart rate accelerates. I talk to myself *a lot* to stay calm, reminding myself that most intelligent people I know enter willingly into a silver tube that jets through the sky, and they are completely confident and peaceful in doing so. I watch the faces of those around me who don't seem to be nervous at all—in fact, some are sound asleep!—and try to mimic their peaceful demeanor. The minute the plane touches down, I am thanking God for another day of life on this planet.

People have tried to help me with this by sharing facts and statistics demonstrating that more people die in car accidents than plane crashes. They offer reassuring statements about planes being able to handle a whole lot more turbulence than what we are experiencing on the flight. And on and on the facts go. But the thing is, at the level of my body and my emotions, I am still afraid! No matter all the reassuring facts I have learned, my palms are still sweating, my heart is still beating wildly, and I can't concentrate on what I'm reading! Knowing the facts helps a little bit, but it is not deeply transforming. I'm still afraid of something that all good reason tells me I needn't be afraid of. Knowing the facts has not transformed my fear. There are deeper levels of my being that would need to be transformed for me to be released from this fear.

This session is designed to guide your group in interacting about the "facts" of spiritual transformation and to provide clarity about the process of moving beyond belief to faith, beyond information to transformation.

READ AND REFLECT

Prior to your meeting, read and reflect on chapters three and four, paying attention to resonance, resistance, stirrings of the Holy Spirit, and questions you are wondering about. Which of the biblical foundations and perspectives do you feel solid resonance with, and which ones surprise you or make you feel uncomfortable? Is there anything you need to study and dig into a little more? Again, you may want to use different colored highlighters to keep track of these experiences, make notes in the margins, or keep a notebook or a journal for ease of sharing when your group gets together.

- Reflect on the difference between belief and faith. How have you experienced this difference in your own life? What does this tell you about the role of the mind in our spiritual transformation?

- Do you agree or disagree that spiritual transformation is central to the message of the gospel and therefore central to the mission of the church? If not, why not? This will be one of the most important truths your group will need to discuss and find unity on as you move forward in becoming a transforming community, so it will be good for you to reflect on this personally as preparation for discussing with your group.

WHEN YOUR GROUP GETS TOGETHER

Sharing and Listening

Share as much or as little as each of you would like from your personal reflections on chapters three and four covering some biblical and theological foundations. It may take a little more discipline to stay focused on the inner dynamics of resonance, resistance, and the stirring of the Spirit in relation to these things. In this section, try your best not to let your sharing devolve into a heady, intellectual conversation. That can come later.

Prayerful Discussion

This discussion will be a little more academic in that you will be covering some of the basic biblical and theological foundations that undergird your journey of becoming a transforming community.

There will be a question for each major topic covered in these two chapters. If you are concerned about time, feel free to choose the questions your group most needs to discuss—probably those that challenge your tradition or where there might be some disagreement.

1. ***Christ formed in us.*** How do you respond to the definition of spiritual transformation offered on page 41 and the distinction made between discipleship and spiritual formation?

2. ***By the renewing of our minds.*** What do you think of when you think about the mind? How do you respond to the Greek definition of the word *nous* that Paul uses to refer to the mind and what this indicates about what is really involved in the process of transformation? Reflect on a change that has taken place in your life or one you would like to see in your life and your awareness that it will take more than learning new facts for it to really change. How does this help you grasp the nature of spiritual transformation as we are defining it here?

3. ***The work of the Spirit.*** What do you personally believe about the Holy Spirit, and how was this shaped in the tradition(s) you have been a part of? How do you experience the Holy Spirit in your life now?

4. ***Embracing mystery.*** How comfortable are you with mystery—that is, something that exists outside the range of human understanding and human agency? When have you experienced the mystery of divine revelation or divine intervention in your own life? How does this help you trust the more mysterious aspects of spiritual transformation?

5. ***The role of spiritual practices.*** Respond together to the idea that spiritual practices are concrete activities we can engage in that open us to the work only God can do. What difference would it make to your discipleship efforts if you understood and believed this? What spiritual practices or rhythms do you have in place that keep you open and available to the transforming work of God in your life? What disciplines are you drawn to experience or learn more about?

6. ***For the sake of others.*** How do you experience your transformation to be "for the sake of others"—or not? When and how do you experience the tension Mulholland describes here?

7. ***Beyond dualisms.*** How have you experienced the false dichotomy between being and doing in your own life and in the tradition that has shaped you? What is your response to the idea of living in

creative tension versus giving in to one polarity or the other, especially as it has to do with loving God and loving neighbor, solitude and engagement with the world, prayer and action?

8. ***Love in a cruciform shape.*** A question leaders often ask is, What is the outcome or "the return on time" for our investment in spiritual transformation? How do we know we are being effective? Chapter four describes cruciform love in its many facets as the outcome of our spiritual transformation. How do you respond to this? How does this emphasis align (or not) with your understanding of the atonement? Is there anything here that needs further study and clarification in your setting?

9. ***The three struggles of discipleship.*** Spend some time reflecting together on the three struggles of discipleship Ron Rolheiser describes on page 66. Share together where you think you might be in your own life relative to these struggles, and where most of your community tends to be. How does looking at your community through this lens help you to "see" more clearly what your community might need for deepening the journey of spiritual transformation?

NEXT STEPS IN TRANSFORMING COMMUNITY

Consider where your community is in their understanding of the biblical and theological foundations for spiritual transformation as central to the message of the gospel and therefore central to the mission of the church. Which of the main theological categories covered in this chapter is your community particularly strong in? Which might need more teaching and input and how can you offer this? What delivery mechanisms—preaching, teaching, educational settings and small groups, leadership training and development, congregational meetings, and so on—can you leverage to establish these foundations? How can you strike a balance between giving enough information so people can feel confident in the direction you're taking but not so much that they become bored with the theoretical?

Here's a hopeful thought: Once you start teaching and casting vision for becoming a transforming community, you might discover that people don't really need that much convincing! You may discover that people are already convinced and have just been waiting for someone to lead the way!

PRAY FOR OUR COMMUNITY

Session 3

SOLITUDE

Living from the Center Out

Without solitude it is virtually
impossible to live a spiritual life.

Henri Nouwen

Paradoxically, transforming community begins in solitude as we center ourselves in God and then live out of that center into community and then into the world. This pattern is seen most clearly at the beginning of Jesus' ministry as recorded in Luke 6:12-19. Jesus went out to the mountain and spent the night in prayer, centering himself in God. Then he moved out from the center and chose his community, and then from there they engaged others with the good news of the gospel and with their healing presence. This is the pattern of transforming community. In this session, we will take an initial look at the concentric circles of relationship in which the spiritual life unfolds, beginning with solitude at the center. We will also consider what it might look like for your community to live intentionally from the center out as a way of arranging your life together for spiritual transformation.

READ AND REFLECT

Prior to your meeting, read and reflect on chapters five and six.

- Consider the concentric circles diagram (page 73) and how you respond to the idea of living from the center out. Is this way of envisioning the spiritual life helpful to you in any way?

- Which of the circles is most well-represented in your life and practice? Which one is "thin" or even missing altogether? What is God saying to you as you observe this together?

- What about your community's life? Which of the circles is robustly supported in the life of your community? Which ones are weak or even missing?

- What is your practice of solitude and silence like right now? What is happening (or not happening) between you and God in that very intimate space? When and where have you had the chance to share silence with others? What has that meant to you, and where might you be able to find that now?

- Where do you find yourself with the idea that honoring the body is a spiritual practice as significant as other "spiritual" practices? Are you resonant? Resistant? Neutral? (Try to stay with this question for yourself first before thinking about your community.) Which of the practices related to this do you already have in place, and which ones do you need or want to consider incorporating?

- This chapter surfaced some of the more complicated issues having to do with life in a body—sex, sexuality, gender, race and ethnicity, illness, aging, mortality, abuse. Is there any aspect of life in *your* body that you have not fully attended to yet? What do you want to say to God about that? Do you have any sense of how you might take next steps in giving this area of your life the attention it needs? Are you willing to see this as part of your own transformational journey as well as part of what it might mean for you to be a transforming leader?

WHEN YOUR GROUP GETS TOGETHER

Sharing and Listening

Share as much or as little as you would like about your personal response to these chapters. After everyone has shared, enter into a prayerful dialogue using the questions below.

Prayerful Discussion

1. As you consider the concentric circles diagram, which practices are most fully developed in your community's life right now? What's missing? Which practices might correspond to the desires your community is expressing?

2. When, where, and how have you experienced the dangers of community without solitude? Discuss specific examples of what human beings cannot do for each other that only God can do. What could it mean to your communal life if you were clearer about the fact that transforming community begins in solitude?

3. When have you experienced sharing silence with others? What was that like? Is there any place where sharing silence happens in your community's life? If not, are you as leaders drawn to this at all? How might you incorporate this?

4. Which of the transformative practices found in the solitude circle—silence, prayer, journaling, fasting, cultivating biblical literacy and contemplative approaches to Scripture, self-examination leading to self-knowledge, celebration, confession, discernment, and so on—are emphasized, well-resourced, and

experienced together in your community's life? Which ones (and maybe others) need to be shored up?

5. Share from your past traditions as well as from the tradition your community is a part of now about whether you have experienced "the ambiguous legacy" Stephanie Paulsell describes around life in our bodies as it relates to our spirituality. Was this addressed positively or negatively or not at all in the traditions you were raised in? How do you experience this in your community now?

6. Where is the goodness of the body taught and experienced in your community? What guidance do you provide to help people integrate the life of the body with the life of the mind and the life of the Spirit, and elevate it to a level of equal importance?

7. What is the pace of life like in your community? Is your community a place where people learn how to establish sane rhythms of work and rest in their lives? How do you teach and practice sabbath together—or not?

8. How, when, and in what contexts do you teach about the connections between sexuality and spirituality?

9. Is there any area in which your community's life discriminates against people based on their physical characteristics and orientations?

10. When, how, and in what contexts do you address bodily experiences such as race, gender, sexual orientation, infertility, differently abled, neurodiversity, chronic and/or terminal illness, a spirituality of death and dying? What can be done to provide resources, shepherding, and pastoral care to those experiencing these aspects of life in a body?

11. What kinds of diversity are represented in your community, and which aspects of diversity are missing? Do you agree or disagree that the most significant levels of transformation take place in diverse communities? What does this say about your community?

12. Are there any topics related to life in our bodies that you have avoided talking about in your community? How do you feel about bringing some of those issues to the forefront as part of your journey of transformation together—especially the more challenging ones like race, gender, and sexuality? Does this seem important to you?

13. Are people—especially women and children—sexually safe in your community? What policies and practices do you have in place that ensure physical safety and/or proper attention when someone's safety has been violated? Is it enough?

NEXT STEPS IN TRANSFORMING COMMUNITY

In this section you are invited to consider what you are already offering that elevates solitude and silence as the place where the spiritual life begins and teaches people how to practice it or whether more is needed. What are some intentional steps you could take toward a more embodied approach to spirituality in your setting, one that affirms our bodies as places of encounter with God? Here are some ideas to prime the pump as you listen for how God might be leading you in taking concrete next steps.

- Preach and/or teach about solitude and silence as the heart of transforming community. Make sure your own practice is substantive enough that you can preach with inner authority that comes from experience.

- Offer a class (Sunday school, Christian education, etc.) or a retreat that gives step-by-step guidance into the practice of solitude and silence and offers the opportunity to debrief experiences and receive support for what gets stirred up. Make sure that the person who is holding the class is qualified to do so; a trained spiritual director would be ideal. Using a resource like *Invitation to Solitude and Silence,* which breaks it down into bite-size practices, would also be very supportive.
- Add silence into your worship services—maybe right after the Scripture reading—to let God speak to souls first, before the sermon. Guide people into this time.
- Offer a regular practice of centering prayer groups and/or lectio divina groups to embed practices that emphasize silence into your community's life.
- Host a congregational retreat once a year that includes less programming and more time in solitude.
- Incorporate more embodiment into your worship services—prayers with gestures, breathing exercises, liturgical movement and dance, and so on.
- Offer classes during the week that provide guidance and practices for living well in our bodies at all stages—yoga, cultivating a healthy relationship with food, support groups for parents of neurodivergent children, exercise classes for the elderly or those who are differently abled, dance classes, and so on.

PRAY FOR OUR COMMUNITY

Session 4

COMMUNITY

Sustaining Us in the Mystery

Left to ourselves we do not have the resources to maintain the disciplines that God uses as means of grace to transform us to wholeness in the image of Christ.

M. Robert Mulholland Jr.

In this session we move from the innermost concentric circle of solitude to our circle of relationships in community. This circle encompasses family, friends, spiritual companions, small groups, church, denomination, and the communion of saints. To launch into this topic, I have been drawn to the Emmaus Road narrative. It might be helpful in making the transition into this topic to read Luke 24:13-36 alone and together, noting what draws your attention and stirs your heart with fresh vision for life together in Christ.

READ AND REFLECT

Prior to your meeting, read and reflect on chapters seven, eight, nine, and ten.

- In what area of your life do you experience yourself to be between the now and the not-yet? What is that like for you? Which aspect of the Emmaus Road narrative connects most meaningfully with your journey right now?

- Reflect on a moment where what you were going through was so awful or so wonderful that you couldn't put it into words even though you wanted to. What happened when you tried to share that with someone? Did they rush in with advice, fixing, problem solving, trite comfort? Or did they give you and "it" space to just be? What did this mean to you?

- Reflect a bit on your varied experiences with worship. What kinds of worship experiences have you found to be transformative, not merely inspirational? What are you longing for in worship these days?

- As you read about stages of faith, what insights did you receive about your own journey through the stages? Did the description of the stages help you make more sense out of some aspect of your own journey?

WHEN YOUR GROUP GETS TOGETHER

Sharing and Listening

Share as much or as little as you would like about your personal response to these chapters. After everyone has shared, enter into a prayerful dialogue using the questions below.

Prayerful Discussion

1. In your community, is there a sense of cohesion around what community is and what it exists to be and to do? Does your community need a picture that is worth a thousand words? A good litmus test for this would be to ask a few random people at different levels of engagement in your community how they define or understand community and see what they say!

2. Talk together about the concept of liminal space. What is your experience of this? How does your community give guidance and support for this unique spiritual position where human beings hate to be, but where God is always calling them?

3. Which of the moments or movements in the walk to Emmaus resonates with where your community is right now or what it might need?

4. What is your community's experience regarding relationships between women and men in the body of Christ? Have you witnessed and experienced the kind of equality and mutuality described in this chapter? How do you respond to the vision for equality and shared leadership among the brothers and the sisters in the family of God as modeled in Jesus' life, especially in the post-resurrection accounts? How might your community practice the kind of mutuality and oneness observed here? Be specific.

5. How familiar is your community with the practice of paying attention to consolation and desolation as a way of discerning the presence of Christ? Is that a level of sharing you are comfortable with in this group? How could you introduce this spiritual practice more widely?

6. Pages 122-24 describe concrete practices we can commit to that help us open to Jesus' transforming presence together. How might these be incorporated into your community's life? Are there one or two that stand out?

7. Review the characteristics of transforming worship described in chapters eight and nine—highly relational (with God), highly participatory, committed to excellence (but not perfection), holistic (engaging the whole person), incorporating corporate practices for surrendering to God such as silence, listening and responding to God in Scripture, transforming preaching, and so on. Which of these stood out to you as something you do well, and which stood out as something you need to cultivate more intentionally?

8. Chapter ten begins by describing the spiritual journey as the journey of surrender. Is your community set up to facilitate this kind of journey? Are people growing in this?

9. Which stages of faith is your community particularly good at supporting? Which ones do you sense need to be resourced more intentionally? Are there any patterns you can observe about where people are at in their spiritual development when they join your community and/or leave your community?

NEXT STEPS IN TRANSFORMING COMMUNITY

Identify concrete next steps you feel called to take in response to your reading and reflections on chapters seven, eight, nine, and ten on practices in community. Since these chapters encompass such significant aspects of your community's life, you may need to take time with each theme, or you could break into at least four smaller groups to wrestle with next steps in four key areas—community practices and covenant regarding how you are inviting people to walk together (chapter seven), transforming worship (chapter eight), life together under the Word (chapter nine), ministry offerings for stages of faith (chapter ten)—and then have the smaller working groups report back to the larger group. You will probably end up with concrete next steps in all four of these areas.

Choosing to walk together. You might want to consider launching a few small groups or teams that meet to experience the spiritual companionship modeled in the walk to Emmaus utilizing *Life Together in Christ.*

Transforming worship. Rory Noland's book *Transforming Worship* would be an excellent resource for the group taking a deeper dive on this.

Engaging Scripture together. Evaluate your group's current rhythms for reading Scripture together, and experiment with other practices such as lectio divina.

Stages of faith. Allot some time for one person or several people on your staff or in your group to dig into the literature on stages of faith and human development and then have them present their findings to the larger leadership group.

Here are some recommended resources that could be the foundation for your exploration: *Invitation to a Journey: A Road Map for Spiritual Formation* (chapter 8) by M. Robert Mulholland; *The Critical Journey: Stages in the Life of Faith* by Janet Hagberg and Robert Guelich; *Stages of Faith: The Psychology of Human Development and the Quest for Meaning* by James Fowler; *Spiritual Pilgrims: Carl Jung and Theresa of Ávila* by John Welsh; *Life Maps: Conversations on the Journey of Faith* by James Fowler and Sam Keen; *Interior Castle* by Theresa of

Ávila; *The Dark Night of the Soul* by Gerald May; *Sacred Fire: A Vision for a Deeper Human and Christian Maturity* by Ron Rolheiser; and *The Cloud of Unknowing* translated by Carmen Acevedo Butcher.

After the presentations, choose one of the models that resonates and fits best in your context, or decide that you want to take everything you've learned and develop your own model using pieces from all the different sources you've studied. (The latter approach is the one I took in one church I served, and it was very helpful to consolidate what I had learned about stages of faith in seminary and beyond into a language that corresponded to what we were already doing, with some additions.)

Once you have identified the stages in a way that fits and resonates in your setting, take time to run through a very simple exercise. Put each stage on a piece of newsprint one at a time and, using bullet points, describe the characteristics of each stage, the needs at each stage, and your assessment of what your community already provides or might need to develop. Your newsprint might look something like this:

> Pre-awareness (or whatever word you are using to describe this stage):
>
> Characteristics:
>
> Needs:
>
> Assessment:
>
> - How does our community currently resource people at this stage of their spiritual journey?
> - What do we still need to develop to support and challenge people at this stage, especially if they get stuck?

Then based on this work, you can come up with concrete next steps.

PRAY FOR OUR COMMUNITY

Session 5

MISSION

In God for the World

All God's work to conform us to
the image of Christ has as its sole purpose that
we might become what God created us to be
in relationship with God and others.

M. ROBERT MULHOLLAND JR.

THE CHURCH HAS A SINGLE BINARY MISSION—to be in God for the world in two contexts: in the corporate context of our life together in Christ and in the social context of our life with others in our cultural context. The outer concentric circle shatters the false dualism that often gets created between formation and mission; it shows that a transforming community is, by definition, missional because being formed in the image of Christ means Christ's love for the world is being formed in us. To encounter the risen Christ on the road between the now and the not-yet is to be sent by him to be bearers and practitioners of the good news. The rhythm of a genuinely Christian spirituality is "not only rooted in a vital, growing relationship with God at the center of one's being but is also incarnated in the reality of the social, economic and political contexts in which one lives. Such spirituality is relevant, revolutionary, transforming" (M. Robert Mulholland Jr. in *Invitation to a Journey*).

READ AND REFLECT

Prior to your meeting, read and reflect on chapters eleven, twelve, and thirteen.

- How do you respond to the distinction Mulholland makes between being "in the world for God" and being "in God for the world"? Can you not only understand but *feel* the difference this would make in how you engage others in your world?

- "God so loved the world that he gave . . ." (John 3:16). Do you have a sense that you are participating in the generosity of God's nature as you share your financial resources, your material possessions, your very self, or would this be something new for you? Is your transformation forming a more generous spirit in you? How do you notice this?

- Where do you sense that forbearing with someone in your life is what God is asking of you? Is there anyone you are resisting forgiving? Are you ready to ask God for the grace to be made willing? Is there anyone you are in the process of forgiving? Where are you in the process?

- How do you respond to the truth that justice is love? How do you personally practice justice? What area of injustice are you most attuned to right now, and how are you contributing to the work of justice in that area?

WHEN YOUR GROUP GETS TOGETHER

Sharing and Listening

Create space for each person to share as much or as little as they would like about their personal reflections on chapters eleven, twelve, and thirteen. Remember this is not a discussion (that will come later), but clarifying questions are welcome.

Prayerful Discussion

1. Discuss the fragility that characterizes us when are trying to find our identity somewhere else besides God. Where do you experience this in your own lives and in the life of your community?

2. Is the distinction between "being in the world for God" or "being in God for the world" a new idea in your setting? What difference would it make to your engagement with the world if your community grasped this?

3. How do you respond to the distinction between "imitation" and "being partakers of the divine nature" (*theosis*)? How would you articulate the difference? Which do you find more inspiring? Why?

4. Take time to discuss the practices that open us to participation in the divine nature. What stands out to you about each one and how do each of these play out in your setting?

- *Generosity:* When and in what contexts do you teach about generosity? Is it just around stewardship Sunday or some sort of capital campaign, or is generosity a thread running throughout your community's life and teaching?

- *Forbearance:* Is forbearance something your community is familiar with and knows how to practice—especially in these divisive times?

- *Forgiveness:* What teaching, guidance, and support for the process does your community offer regarding the practice of forgiveness? What resources are available or recommended (i.e., pastoral care and counseling, spiritual direction, trauma-based therapy, examples given from the pulpit, etc.) to aid in this process, given how significant forgiveness is from a spiritual point of view?

5. Invite each person to share which practice feels most challenging yet perhaps most needed in their lives right now. Which one(s) do you think might need to be taught and emphasized more fully in your community?

6. What do you think about Richard Rohr's statement that liberation is the largest frame in which to understand spirituality and that it is at the heart of the Christian message (page 194)? How might a clearer understanding of this impact your community's life and your engagement with the issues of the day?

7. At the beginning of chapter thirteen, I share the beginnings of my own justice journey, how that journey has unfolded over time, and how it has shaped our community. Share your own justice journeys with each other and where you are on that journey right now.

8. Reflect on your journey as a community. Is a commitment to justice something that characterizes your community in ways that are easily recognizable? Are there ways in which your community could be more intentional about loving what God loves (see Isaiah 61:8)?

NEXT STEPS IN TRANSFORMING COMMUNITY

Now is your opportunity to translate your discussion into concrete next steps. Resist feeling overwhelmed; determine to do something before you do everything and be realistic about how much you can do at once. As you list next steps, be sure to record the name or names of who is responsible next to each item.

PRAY FOR OUR COMMUNITY

Session 6

DISCERNING A TRANSFORMING WAY OF LIFE IN COMMUNITY

The church is like a swimming pool in which all the noise comes from the shallow end. But most of the wisdom is to be found in the deep end, among those who have taken time and cultivated the habits and disciplines to learn to swim in deeper waters. If we are to love God with all our heart, soul, mind, and strength, then we need the kind of sustained learning that leads us into the deep end of the pool.

William H. Vanstone

Saint Benedict was the first to develop a "rule of life" to help the monks living together under his care to order their lives very simply around three key elements of their life in God: prayer, study, and work. Saint Bendict's rule, like any rule of life, was a communal pattern of attitudes (postures), behaviors, and practices that were regular and routine, intended to produce a certain quality of life and character in those who followed it. As the abbot of twelve monasteries, Saint Benedict developed his rule around fifteen hundred years ago, and the use of his rule spread to hundreds of monasteries across Europe in the Middle Ages. While its language and cultural references might seem somewhat stilted and overly authoritarian to us, the concept of sharing a way of life that is intended to open us to God's transforming work still holds as it continues to grow and evolve to meet the spiritual desires of our day. As Benedict writes in the prologue to his rule, we are invited to accept a rule of life (or sacred rhythms) with willing freedom, emerging from prayer as love responds to love. The heart of it all is seeking to respond to God's love in every moment of our lives.

This final session is your opportunity to think, pray, and reflect about how you can arrange your life together for spiritual transformation.

READ AND REFLECT

Prior to your meeting, read and reflect on chapter fourteen plus the epilogue.

- Reflect once again on the question of whether spiritual transformation is elective or essential. Has your understanding of this distinction deepened in any way and how do you respond to that question now?

- How do you think your community as a whole understands this?

- Reflect on the role of leadership in transforming community and especially the idea that the best thing we bring to leadership is our own transforming self. Do you feel prepared to provide leadership for transforming community from a place of inner authority?

- As you reflect on the graphic titled "How spiritual transformation happens in the life of a person" on page 221, does it resonate with your experience of your own transformation and what you've witnessed in the lives of others?

- Do you personally have the vision and the energy to be a leader in the process of becoming a transforming community?

WHEN YOUR COMMUNITY GETS TOGETHER

Sharing and Listening

Invite each person to share as much or as little as they would like about their personal response to these chapters. Focus on creating space for each person to share and for the group to receive that sharing versus getting too deep into the discussion just yet. Clarifying questions, affirmations, and gratitude for what each person has offered to the group are all appropriate here.

Prayerful Discussion

After everyone has shared, begin a dialogue using these questions as a guide.

1. Discuss together the all-important question of whether you agree that spiritual transformation is essential rather than elective. Do not move on until you have a clear sense of where your group is on this question. If everyone agrees that the answer is yes, it is essential, what changes might this necessitate for your community? What other priorities might need to be shifted?

2. How do you respond to the idea that spiritual transformation as the Spirit of God working deep and fundamental changes in the life of the individual needs to be modeled at every level of leadership in your community? Are you up for this?

3. Discuss the graphic titled "How spiritual transformation happens in the life of a person" on page 221. How does this fit with your growth and discipleship model? Note what seems similar and what might need additional merging and/or development.

4. Discuss the graphic that illustrates how spiritual transformation can take place in a community and how you might cultivate shared understanding, shared experience, and shared commitment at all levels of your community's life, working from the center out.

5. Consider your statement of values (if you have one) and whether it reflects your commitment to spiritual transformation as central to the message of the gospel and therefore central to the mission of your community. Are there values you need to add? (The Transforming Center statement of values is found in the appendix of *Leading a Transforming Community*. You may want to refer to it as an example.)

6. Add a concrete practice or two to each value, so they become more than just nice-sounding ideas.

7. Would you say that your community is busy and burned out, or is it characterized by incarnational living? How can you move more in the direction of incarnational living where the Spirit and the energy of Christ are flowing through you and always being replenished?

8. Reflect together on the final question put forth in the epilogue: Can the institutionalized church or institutions of any kind be transforming communities? Are we able to distinguish between the institution and the actual living, breathing, growing body of Christ on the earth now? What is it about the process of becoming an institution that makes it harder to change and transform?

9. How do you respond to the idea that certainty is the great enemy of unity? What might it mean for our faith to be a living thing that walks hand in hand with doubt as we cultivate transforming community?

NEXT STEPS IN TRANSFORMING COMMUNITY

Work through the On the Road to Becoming a Transforming Community tool in the appendix, noting the places where more intention and planning are needed. Let your next steps emerge from what you observe through working with this document. (You may want to schedule an additional meeting for this, as it is very substantive and may take quite a bit of discussion to agree on where you are in the categories outlined.)

PRAY FOR OUR COMMUNITY

Appendix

ON THE ROAD TO BECOMING A TRANSFORMING COMMUNITY

A Tool for Gentle Noticing

I am again in the pain of childbirth until Christ is formed in you.

Galatians 4:19

Spiritual transformation is the process by which Christ is formed in us for the glory of God, for the abundance of our own lives, and for the sake of others. A transforming community is men and women journeying together in the presence of Christ for the purpose of spiritual transformation so we can discern and do the will of God.

Following are statements that capture some of the core commitments of a transforming community. As you reflect on each one, gently notice where your community is on the road to understanding, embracing, and living out these core commitments at the present time, and indicate that on each continuum accordingly. This is not for the purpose of judging your situation harshly but rather to offer a way of naming current reality so you can move more intentionally toward the vision of becoming a transforming community.

Enter into this reflection prayerfully, remembering that Jesus loves the church, his body on the earth now, and he loves *your* community—a unique expression of his love and presence in the setting where he has placed you. He longs to lead you lovingly into the reality of kingdom living here and now.

TRANSFORMATION IN CHRIST'S PRESENCE

1. ***Shared understanding.*** Our community has developed a shared biblical and Christocentric understanding of spiritual transformation—what it is, how it happens in the life of a person, the role of spiritual disciplines, etc.

Always Often Sometimes Rarely Never

2. ***Shared experience.*** Our community is having shared experiences with the spiritual practices, relationships, and experiences that open us to God's transforming work. This includes practices that take place in concentric circles of relationship—solitude (alone with God), community (with God with others), and the world beyond our community (in God for the world).

Always Often Sometimes Rarely Never

3. ***Shared commitment.*** Our community affirms together that spiritual transformation in Christ's presence is central to the message of the gospel and therefore central to the mission of the church to the extent that it is an organizing principle.

Always Often Sometimes Rarely Never

4. ***Alignment.*** In all facets of our life together, we are working proactively toward being aligned around the language, priority, and process of spiritual transformation. This includes all "ministry" areas (worship, preaching and teaching, Christian education, missions and outreach, community life, pastoral care) as well as operations, production and programming, human resources, financial practices, building and grounds, etc.

Always Often Sometimes Rarely Never

5. ***Stages of faith.*** We are committed to working wisely with individuals and groups through a growing understanding of the stages

of faith and human development, supporting and resourcing them at all stages.

Always Often Sometimes Rarely Never

6. ***Holistic.*** We are committed to an integrated approach to formation, addressing all aspects of the human person including spirituality, sexuality, psychology, the body, and the brain (neuroscience).

Always Often Sometimes Rarely Never

COMMUNITY

7. ***Community as the context for transformation.*** We are seeing a growing commitment to community as the context in which our spiritual transformation takes place as we participate in the body of Christ here on this earth.

Always Often Sometimes Rarely Never

8. ***How we treat one another matters.*** We agree together that the quality of our relationships is a significant factor in each person's formation. We are committed to values, principles, and relational practices that are transforming rather than deforming; we know that when we violate our community relationships, we are compromising our very essence.

Always Often Sometimes Rarely Never

9. ***Equality, mutuality, and unity in diversity.*** In the community of Jesus, we welcome one another, include one another, and receive one another's gifts without regard to race, gender, or socioeconomic status.

Always Often Sometimes Rarely Never

10. ***Fruit of the Spirit.*** We are seeing increasing evidence of the Spirit's work in relationships in community and beyond our

community—more love, faith, patience, gentleness, kindness, generosity, direct communication with truth and grace, patience, confession, forgiveness, peace, etc. In other words, we are growing up in every way into Christ!

Always Often Sometimes Rarely Never

11. ***Increasing self-knowledge through self-examination and confession.*** Since spiritual transformation takes place primarily in those places where we are not like Christ, we are guiding our community in practices that foster a greater awareness of those places where we are not like Christ; we provide tools and support for self-examination; and we model and practice confessing our sins to one another—privately (before God), interpersonally (with others), and corporately (public worship)—so that we may be healed.

Always Often Sometimes Rarely Never

12. ***Conflict transformation.*** We have clear guidelines and practices in place for opening to the transforming presence of Christ in the midst of conflict. We are committed to working for and maintaining unity—to the best of our ability—as a way of loving Jesus and honoring his desire that we would experience unity.

Always Often Sometimes Rarely Never

SACRED RHYTHMS

13. ***Personal rhythms/rule of life.*** We are consistently and intentionally working toward the goal that each leader and member of our community can articulate and embrace a personal rule of life that is life-giving and keeps them open to the process of transformation.

Always Often Sometimes Rarely Never

14. ***Communal rhythms/rule of life.*** We have developed (or are developing) a rule of life in community that helps us open to God

together through a balanced rhythm of spiritual transformation, discerning the will of God, and doing the will of God (mission). We make scheduling decisions in such a way that we model, guide, and support individuals and families in establishing sane rhythms of work and rest, solitude and community, prayer and action.

Always — Often — Sometimes — Rarely — Never

15. ***Rhythms of the church year.*** We are committed to living intentionally within the rhythms of the church year and are experiencing them as seasons of transformation.

Always — Often — Sometimes — Rarely — Never

TRANSFORMING LEADERSHIP

16. ***Working from the center out.*** We believe the best thing anyone brings to leadership is their own transforming self, so each leader in our community is committed to an ongoing, intentional process of spiritual transformation. Thus, spiritual transformation is being taught, lived, and modeled by individuals at all levels of leadership.

Always — Often — Sometimes — Rarely — Never

17. ***Working with systems.*** We understand that every church or ministry is a living system in which each person's family of origin and other psychological patterns are played out. Leaders are taking responsibility for their own self-differentiation and are working on their own psychological health and wholeness as a way of impacting the system in a positive way.

Always — Often — Sometimes — Rarely — Never

DISCERNMENT AS A WAY OF LIFE TOGETHER

18. ***Personal discernment.*** Individuals are being taught and are growing in their commitment to discern and do the will of God

in their personal decision-making with the help of spiritual companions.

Always Often Sometimes Rarely Never

19. ***Corporate leadership discernment.*** Leadership groups at all levels are committed to discerning God's will together regarding important decisions and are discovering concrete practices for doing so.

Always Often Sometimes Rarely Never

20. ***Discernment in community.*** The congregation is invited into discernment processes regarding important matters in the community's life, in ways appropriate to church polity and structure. Strong teaching and guidance are provided for how to participate effectively in communal discernment and structure. If our church polity is not set up to allow for effective discernment together, we are willing to challenge and/or consider ways of restructuring ourselves so we can carry out this important function of transforming community.

Always Often Sometimes Rarely Never

FOR THE SAKE OF OTHERS

21. ***Spiritual formation and missional engagement with the world.*** We understand spiritual transformation as a valuable end in itself and as a prerequisite to discerning how we are to be "in God for the world" Jesus loves and gave his life for. We are responding to God's unique call to specific and tangible ministries in the world while at the same time living within the sacred rhythms that will sustain us for kingdom action. [You may want to list the specific, tangible ministries your community feels called to at this time.]

Always Often Sometimes Rarely Never

22. ***Commitment to justice.*** Our community reflects deeply on justice issues as one aspect of God's nature that we are to participate in. We don't just preach and teach about justice; we discern ways of getting involved that are appropriate to our setting and the cultural moment in which we live.

Always Often Sometimes Rarely Never

23. ***Do no harm.*** We have developed a theology and praxis of power that is resulting in a growing ability to use power (both positional power and inner authority), limiting the abuse of power in our setting.

Always Often Sometimes Rarely Never

TRANSFORMING | Resources®

Transforming Worship

Spiritual Disciplines Handbook

Invitations from God

The Deeper Journey

Invitation to a Journey

To learn more about transforming resources, communities, and events, visit

transformingcenter.org